# THE LEGEND OF THE
# *Christmas Trees*

THOMAS ANONYMOUS

Copyright © 2019 by Thomas Anonymous.

ISBN  Softcover     978-1-951469-24-5

All rights reserved. No part of this book may be reproduced or transmitted in any form or by any means, electronic or mechanical, including photocopying, recording, or by any information storage and retrieval system without express written permission from the author, except in the case of brief quotations embodied in critical reviews and certain other non-commercial uses permitted by copyright law.

Printed in the United States of America.

To order additional copies of this book, contact:
**Bookwhip**
1-855-339-3589
https://www.bookwhip.com

JOE COULD HARDLY WAIT to go into sixth grade. The teacher was a neighbor of his, and she had a big collie dog that she brought to school with her every day. He could imagine himself petting the dog and playing with it every day. Some of the kids in sixth grade told Joe they were studying about dinosaurs. Joe was fascinated with them, and he didn't want to wait to get started studying about them. He didn't care about sports or playing games outdoors at recess, He really liked to play marbles, and he was getting pretty good at it.

One day, in December, when Joe came in his room after recess, he felt his leg getting very cold under his right pocket. He had been playing with the marbles in the snow, and had picked them up in a hurry, and stuffed them in his pocket. He pulled the pooner(a marble that is bigger than the others)out of his pocket and was surprised to see that it was still covered with snow. Joe wasn't thinking about very much. He just wanted to get rid of the snow and stuff the marbles back in his pocket before Mrs. Madden, his teacher, came back into the classroom. Quickly, Joe popped the pooner, with the snow on it into his mouth, and started to suck the snow off of it. **GULP**! The snow went down, and the pooner went with it! The only thing was, the pooner didn't go all the way down. It was stuck there in his throat and it wouldn't go up or down. Joe couldn't get his breath and he was starting to panic. He was beginning to turn blue.

Desperate, he didn't know what to do. Just then, Mrs. Madden walked through the door. As fast as he could, Joe got out of his seat, and staggered toward her, all the time trying to pat himself on the back.

Joe had almost reached Mrs. Madden, when the pooner popped out of his throat.

To his amazement, Joe caught it. What a relief it was, just to be able to breath. For the next several minutes, Joe just stood there with Mrs. Madden, thinking how good it was just to be alive.

It was a teachable moment for the whole class. Everyone was paying close attention. Mrs. Madden explained to them how they could double up their fist, place it on their stomach and pull in hard, to dislodge anything stuck in their own throat. She also told them they could help someone else who was choking, by getting behind them if they're standing up, and doing the same thing. If they were not, she said to just push on the person's stomach. She warned them to let the person having difficulty breathing know you are going to help them, so they won't be afraid. She also said it was important to put their hands on the person's stomach, and not their chest when helping them. She called this the Heimlich maneuver.

It was about a week later. Joe was eating his supper, one Friday evening, when the phone rang. "It's for you, Joe," his mom said, after a couple of minutes. Joe took the phone. A few minutes later, he said to his folks, "It's Grampa Hayden, he wants me to come over tomorrow and Sunday to help him," Joe said. "Mrs. Julia's going to throw you in the furnace," Joe's Mom said with a chuckle. "I understand now," Joe said, after a long minute. "Grampa said I could go to church with him an' Gram, Sunday. OK if I go?" he continued. "Sure," said his mom, "I'll pack your gym bag."

Joe could remember all too well, what his mother was joking about. It happened this way: One Sunday morning not long before that, Joe's Mom announced that the family would not be going to church, because they were going to their Grandparents' house for the day. "But I gotta go to Sunday School," Joe said. "No," insisted his Mother. "We're going to your Grandparents'!" By now Joe was crying. "I gotta go to Sunday School, I gotta go to Sunday school," he blurted out.

Joe's Mom took a deep breath, got up, and went over to Joe, and gently laid her hands on his shoulders. "Tell me why it's so important to go to Sunday School today," she asked him softly. Joe was sobbing repeatedly. "Cuz, 'cuz," he stammered, "cuz if I miss one more Sunday, Mrs. Julia's goin' 'ta throw me in the furnace," he told her.

"I can't believe that Mrs. Julia would ever say that!" his mother exclaimed. I'm going to call her up right now and find out!"

"All I told the children," Mrs. Julia explained, after a long pause, "was that if they missed three Sundays I was going to drop them from the register."

Joe and his family attended a very old church that heated with a coal furnace, located in the center of the building, in the basement. Covering the top of the furnace, which was at floor level in the church, was a big metal grate, or register, on which Joe and his friends stood many times, warming themselves. By looking down, they could see the red hot coals in the furnace. Joe was not aware that there were two kinds of registers. One for keeping records, and one to cover the top of a furnace or other opening.

Bright and early the next morning, Grampa's truck rolled into the driveway. Grampa came in, sat down and talked with Joey's folks. He was a tall, good-natured man with a handlebar mustache, and spry. After a few minutes, Grampa cleared his throat, and said, "You 'bout ready, Joe?"

"Whoops, I forgot to brush my teeth. I'll be just a minute," Joe replied over his shoulder, as he headed for the bathroom. "Do a good job on those teeth," Grampa called out after him. "You want to keep 'em as long as you can." Joe was back in a few minutes, pulled on his overshoes and jacket, and picked up his gym bag.

"You'll want your hat and mittens," Grampa reminded him.

"They're in the gym bag," his Mom said. Joe gave his folks a quick hug, and Grandson and Grandfather were out the door.

"WOW, you got a new double cab!" Joe exclaimed. "Yup," Grampa replied, "needed to keep my tools and stuff dry. "Toss your gym bag in on the back seat," he continued.

Joe lost track of the time. The new truck hummed along, mile after mile. Grampa wanted to know everything about Joe. He asked what Joe was studying in school, what he and his friends were doing for fun, and what was going on around town. After a long time, Grampa turned off onto a side road that Joe was not familiar with.

"Where are we going, Grampa?" Joe wanted to know.

"To get a Christmas tree," he replied. In a few minutes, Grampa turned his truck onto another road. There were potholes everywhere.

"How come there's so many bumps in this road Grampa?" Joe asked.

"That's because it's a private road, and the town doesn't help with the upkeep."

"Oh," said Joe.

After a long way, the truck turned onto a narrow driveway that went steeply uphill. At the top of the hill was an old, almost square farmhouse. The driveway continued around the farmhouse. Behind the house, and a long way back, was a huge red barn. Grandpa drove to the side of the barn, where there was a small door, and parked the truck. Joe was surprised when they walked in, because it was warm, and the floor was swept clean. On the side of the wall was an old wooden table with several wooden chairs clustered around it. In the middle of the floor was a round, black iron stove, that was almost as tall as Joe. The middle of the stove was bigger around than the rest of it. His Grandfather told Joe later, that they called that a "pot-bellied stove." Inside the barn was an old man with a scruffy beard, wearing a one piece pair of tattered overalls. He was leaning on a cane and puttering around the barn.

Joe was surprised that the two men knew each other.

"That you, Carl?" the old man asked Grampa. "Almost didn't recognize ya with that mustache," he said jokingly.

"Hi, Horace," Joe's Grandfather shot back. "There's a story that goes with that mustache," he chuckled. " I had about two weeks' worth of growth on that," he began, "and one of the women in the church came up to me, and got right in my face. 'You growin' one them things?' she demanded to know. "I told her, yup, I was growin' one them things."

"My husband grew one them things," she said, "an I told my husband, you grow one them things, an' I'll never kiss you again as long as I live...*'an I never did*!"

Horace roared with laughter. "The old guy probably got the best end of that deal," Horace concluded.

"How 'ya been, Horace?" Joe's grandfather wanted to know. "Fair 'ta middlin," Horace replied. "Ya know, some fellas look downright stupid with 'them things', but you look really good with yours! Who's that guy with ya?"

"This is my Grandson, Joe," his Grandfather announced proudly.

"It's a good thing ya brought him," Horace continued, "if ya want a tree this year. I've sold all the ones I pre-cut, so you'll hafta cut one yourselves."

"Oh, sugar!" Joe's Grandfather blurted out, snapping his fingers. "I forgot my saw!"

"Use mine," Horace offered. "I sharpened 'er last night."

"Whew," Grampa sighed, "That'll be fun."

Horace passed Grampa his bow saw with a smile. "OK Joe, Grampa said, "Let's go get us a Christmas tree."

"Be sure and give Joe time to have a hot chocolate, after you tucker him out," said Horace, as the two of them went out the door. "OK said Grampa, put the coffee pot on for me, too."

It was beginning to warm up a bit as Joey and his Grandfather trudged through the snow. It was very quiet except for an occasional chickadee calling to them. There was a dusting of snow still clinging to the tree branches. There were many trees to choose from. Most of them about the same size, around eight or ten feet tall. Occasionally, they would notice one several feet taller than the others. On a hillside, across a little ravine, there were dozens of little Christmas trees growing. "Those won't be ready to cut for another six or eight years," Grampa explained.

"Look, Joe," Grampa said, pointing to a number of small holes in the snow. "Those are deer tracks. Keep your eyes open," he continued, you'll probably see one of the deer peeking out from behind a tree, checking us out."

After several more minutes of closely looking at different trees for shape, Grampa spotted one he liked. "This one's got a lot of lower branches, so your Grandmother can have some fir boughs to decorate with. Saw it off as close to the ground as you can, and I'll put a little pressure on the top, so it won't bind. Can you handle the saw?" Grampa pulled an old pair of gloves out of his pocket and handed them to Joey.

"Here," he said, "put these on, so you won't get your hands all pitch." Joey put the gloves on, got down on his knees, and took the bow saw from his grandfather. He lifted up a lower branch and started to climb under the tree. Suddenly Joey flung the saw wildly off to the side, and scrambled to his feet. "There's a bunny under there!" He exclaimed. "He just went down a hole under the tree."

Grampa slowly got down on his knees and crawled under the branches. "You're right Joe," he said softly, "There's probably a whole family of rabbits in that hole.

The one you saw was most likely out for breakfast," he said as he got on his feet and was brushing himself off.

"What was he eating for breakfast? "Joey wanted to know, as he looked around the tree. "I don't see any grass, or clover, or anything else," he observed.

"See those little twigs, poking out of the snow?" Grampa asked.

"Yeah," said Joey.

"Go snip off one of the ends of one of those twigs." Grampa directed.

Joey did what his grandfather had asked him to. There was a little round nubble on the end of the twig, and Joey brought it back to Grampa. Grampa held the twig with one hand, and pinched the end of the twig with the other. It was green inside.

"To a bunny," Grampa explained, "that's a juicy green salad. Some birds eat those ends, too, like partridges, and birds that can't find bugs to eat." Joey was so amazed, he couldn't speak. He just stood there in wonderment.

"Let's go find us another tree," Grampa suggested. If we cut this one down, the rabbit's den will be exposed, so foxes, hawks and other animals can spot it easily, and have the bunnies for breakfast," he smiled. Joey thought that was a good bit of advice and picked up the bow saw. It wasn't long before Grampa had found another tree to suit him, and the two of them made short work of cutting it and carrying it back to Grampa's truck. "Bring the bow saw into the barn with you, Joe, somebody'll be along and need it too," he explained.

"Still got ya gloves on, huh," Horace said to Joey, when they walked into the barn. "Pitch is a nuisance for us," he said, "but many years ago the pitch on balsam fir trees was *very* expensive. Sit over here, Joe, and enjoy the hot chocolate I just made. How do ya take your coffee, Carl?"

"Black," Carl answered. "I didn't know that about Balsam fir pitch," Joey's Grandfather said. I had heard that thousands of years ago, people used to cut fir boughs and take them inside to make their houses smell good. What did the old timers use the pitch for?"

"I'm not sure about everything," Horace continued, "but I suspect it was used for cosmetics, religious "stuff," and embalming. The Coptic Christian church in Egypt is still using it. Records show that somewhere around Thirty BC, Queen Cleopatra of Egypt traveled all the way to Palestine and brought a whole bunch of cuttings from a Balsam fir grove in Jericho back to Egypt with her. She had them planted in a little town near Cairo called Materia," he continued. "She brought a number of Jewish arborists(or tree farmers) back to Egypt with her, to actually plant and care for the trees. The Jewish tree farmers established a colony at Materia. It's believed that The Holy Family(Mary, Joseph and Jesus) stayed with them while they were in Egypt."

"I got 'ta thinkin' the other day," Horace mused. "It had to be quite a project gettin' ready to travel to Egypt, especially with a young child. Joseph would have had to trade in his donkey toward a camel. They can travel several days in the desert without water, where a donkey can't. Water had to be carried in animal skin bags and food too. They would have had to hook up with a caravan of traders who knew the way. Ya just don't strike off in the desert without knowin' where yer goin'!"

"Traders?" asked Joe.

"Almost everything, except the bare necessities people used, came from somewhere else," Horace explained. "Silks, clothing, tea and spices came from as far away as India and China. Egypt traded a lot of dates and very ornate gold jewelry," he continued.

"The Shetlanders, way up in the North Sea, were trading walrus hides and dried fish, with Europeans," Joe's grandfather added.

"What were walrus hides used for?" Joe wanted to know.

"The military preferred them for shields," his grandfather explained. "They were lightweight and an arrow or sword could not penetrate them."

"Oh, wow!" Joe exclaimed.

"You've seen Oriental rugs, Joe," Horace went on. "Copper was also traded for tools and weapons of war. You've probably heard about Solomon's copper mines at Sunday School." Joe shook his head that he hadn't.

"Religious items from Egypt have been found in ancient Ireland," Horace added, "so Joseph probably didn't have to wait very long to find traders to accompany them in traveling to Egypt."

"There's a legend that goes like this," Horace continued.

"In a little garden, near Materia, where they say the Holy Family stopped to rest, two springs of pure water bubbled up where Jesus' feet first touched the ground. That's very unusual in Egypt, because most spring water there has to be filtered, and purified, to drink. The Balsam Fir grove is gone now, as are the

Jewish tree farmers, but the two little springs are still bubbling away. Another legend around Materia is, that whenever Jesus went by a temple in Egypt, all the idols fell down. There were about twelve hundred different false gods the Egyptians worshipped, and of course there were many temples to those gods. One temple to their sun god lies buried in the sand close by Materia."

Horace cleared his throat again. "Nobody can say for sure that the Holy Family stayed with the tree farmers in Materia while they were in Egypt," Horace said, standing up to stretch. "As time goes on, stories die with the people, but the odds are pretty good that that's where they stayed."

Just then, another customer came into the barn, and Horace had to 'tend to them.' Grampa and Joe got in the truck and headed down the hill.

"Did you know any of that legend, Joe?" Grampa asked.

"No," said Joe, "and I don't think my Sunday School teacher, Mrs. Julia, does either or she would have told us about it. How about you Grampa?"

"I didn't know anything about Queen Cleopatra," Grampa replied, then added. "but I remember reading a book by an English archaeologist by the name of Sir Harry Rimmer, who did a lot of work in Egypt years ago. He identified over a thousand idols that they worshiped."

"Awesome," said Joe. "That's a lot of 'em."

"That's what Rimmer said," Grampa responded. "Let's see," he went on. "There was the sun god Amon Ra, that we talked about, and there were several other sun gods too, like the one with the man's body and a falcon's head. There were a lot of Nile River gods too, which the people appealed to because if the Nile didn't overflow it's banks every year, I understand many people starved to death."

"Wow!" exclaimed Joe, "They'd want as much help as they could get when that happened!"

"That's right," agreed Grampa. There were also cow gods, snake gods, fly and beetle gods, and the one I think is funny, Grampa added chuckling, was the frog god, Hegt, who was supposed to be the fertility god. That one hopped in bed with them, according to the Bible in Exodus. "That's funny," laughed Joe. "I can't wait to tell Mrs. Julia and all the kids in my class in Sunday School.'"

Joe and his grandfather arrived at Joe's grandparent's home just in time to see his Grandmother take a big golden Jonny cake out of the oven. In a few minutes they were all sitting down to a bowl of hot soup and a big piece of Jonny cake.

Joe's Grandmother was interested in the rabbit. She had never heard the legend of the Christmas trees, either.

She was a feisty little lady with her hair pulled straight back in a pug, and she had long bony fingers with big deformed knuckles. Joe had learned long ago that when she wagged her index finger under his nose, he'd better pay attention, and move.

When he was seven or eight, Joe and a neighborhood boy about his age, were playing upstairs in his grandparents' barn. They found an old trunk with women's dresses in it. They thought it would be fun to dress up in the dresses so they did. When they went in the house to show Joe's grandmother, she got very upset. "You boys take those dresses off ***right now***," she demanded, "and you put them back where you got them. ***Now move!***"

Joe's mother laughed when she told Joe of the time she was staying at his grandparent's house, before she had married Joe's father. She was a nurse and had been working nights and had apparently come in, in the night, and crawled into Joe's aunt's bed and went to sleep. Sometime in the morning, Joe's grandmother came into the room and mistook his mother for his aunt. Joe's mother said, "she yanked the bedclothes off me, and gave me a hard slap on the behind, saying, 'Get up! You're not going to sleep all day. There's work to be done!'"

"I'll never forget the look on her face when she realized it was me she had slapped!"

I'm stuffed!" exclaimed Joe, after he had polished off a second smaller piece of Jonny cake. "Me too," said Grampa. "I'm goin' ta have ta have a power nap after all that!" he exclaimed, as he settled into his favorite rocking chair. "There's some old National Geographics over in the corner, there, Joe. I won't be long." Joe's grandmother had gone directly into the other room. Joe wasn't sure what she was doing, but she was very quiet. It wasn't long before his grandfather was snoring away contentedly. Joe checked out the old National Geographics and was imagining himself in some of the African countries pictured on the pages. Probably twenty minutes had gone by when Joe's Grandfather woke himself up with a loud snore. He stood up slowly, stretched, and said, "Ready to go to work, Joe?" Joe was ready and eager to get started. He grabbed his jacket and headed for the door. "Just bring the gloves," Grampa said. "You won't need the jacket, 'cuz the shop's warm."

Joey helped his Grandfather bring the tree into the shop. "I'm going to try and cut the butt off straight. You hold the tree off the floor while I do that," Joey's grandfather said. "There," he said, after that was done. "Your Grandmother's got enough boughs to make a wreath for the front door. She goes over to the church, and helps them make garlands for the windows, but they've got plenty of boughs there for that."

"What are garlands?" Joey wanted to know.

"Those long strings of small boughs that they hang around the church windows. They really dress the place up, and it smells wonderful," Grampa explained.

"Now, while you still have the gloves on, grab one of those boards standing in the corner, over there. I need to have you measure off two small pieces about as long as a candy bar. The tape measure and the square are in the toolbox, on the workbench. Can you do that?" he asked.

"Yup, no problem," said Joe. After he had finished doing that, Joe took the two pieces and put them on the workbench.

"Good job, Joe," his Grandfather said approvingly. "Now we need two of those same boards, about two feet long," he continued. "Measure 'em and get 'em squared off, and I'll hold 'em while you cut 'em." Measuring the boards and squaring them off kept Joe busy for a while. Eventually he brought the two boards to his Grandfather for approval. "I'll hold the boards on the saw horse, while you cut 'em. Be careful!"

When that was done, Grampa told Joe to take one of the boards and nail one of the little pieces on each end of it, and on the same side. "The nails are in that little bag on the work bench. "Good!" he exclaimed. "Now, lay the other board on the floor."

After Joe had done that, his Grandfather said, "Turn the board you nailed the little pieces to upside down and lay it over the board on the floor. Make 'em into a big "X", he said. "OK, good, now nail the two boards together, using the same nails to do it.

"There," he said after Joe had nailed the two pieces together. "The base is done! Now we gotta hook it onto the tree."

Grampa had put a drill bit into the drill. He picked the cross piece up and asked Joe to hold it for him while he drilled a hole all the way through the middle of the base.

"Now," Joe's Grandfather said. "Put the gloves back on and hold the base of the tree up off the floor for me." With that, Grampa drilled a hole in the center of the base. It was about an inch deep. He rummaged around on the work bench for a little while and finally came up with a spike. It was about eight inches long.

"There, Joe, see if you can fit that spike through the hole I drilled in the base we made." The spike went through the hole easily. Grampa had Joe fit the point of the spike into the hole he had drilled in the base of the tree. "See if you can drive the spike into the tree, all the way," he said. "I'll hold the tree while you're doing it." Joe got the spike driven all the way in. Then, Grampa took the hammer and gave the spike one final whack and stood the tree up on the stand.

"Wow," said Joe, that's neat!" Grampa gave Joe a big smile. "You're right," he said, "but we're not done yet. We still have to brace it. It's a lot of extra work, but if the tree falls over the first time the cat climbs up on it, we're right back where we were when we started. There's some narrow boards standing up in the corner, over there, Joe," Grampa said. "We're going to need four of them, about a foot and a half long. Wanna see if you can find any of them for us?" It took Joey all of two minutes to locate four narrow boards. They were not the same length, so he cut each of them the to be same.

Grampa took the four narrow boards, and after adjusting his skill saw, he cut each of the ends at an angle. Then Grampa put a very small bit in his electric hand drill and drilled a little hole in each end of the boards he had cut.

"Joe,", he said, "Grab the hammer out of the tool box, and use some of those small nails you used before, and nail each of the little boards to the tree and the stand. I'll hold the tree while you're doing it. You can get up and down easier than I can. Take your time. The little holes I drilled will keep the boards from splitting when you drive a nail in them. Good, we're done!"

Joe's Grandmother had already placed a large plastic garbage bag on the floor where she wanted the tree to go. "It's beautiful," she said. "We'll decorate it tomorrow after church."

"You timed that right," she jokingly said to Joe's Grandfather. "I'll have supper ready in a little while."

And what a supper it was. She had a big pot of baked beans, a pan of yeast rolls, cole slaw with raisins, and apple pie. Joe had all he could do to move after eating some of everything, however, he did manage to help Grampa wipe dishes after they finished eating. Gram turned the kitchen lights off, and everyone went into the living room where the Christmas tree was. It didn't take Grampa long before he was snoozing in his rocking chair. Gram sat on the couch and took up her knitting. Samantha, the cat, hopped up beside her and cuddled down. Joe was seated on the couch, beside Gram and Samantha. Pretty soon, Joe walked over to the window, and looked out. It was a clear cold night. "I can see the north star," he told Gram.

"People have used that star to navigate by for thousands of years," she explained.

"Which one's the Star of Bethlehem?" Joe wanted to know. For a long minute, Gram kept knitting. Then she cleared her throat and laid her knitting down. "Actually, Joe," she began, "The Star of Bethlehem was not just one star, but several of them that appeared to cluster inside one constellation. Then, they all moved together across the heavens, leading the Wise Men to Jesus.

"Wow, that's awesome!" exclaimed Joe. "I didn't know that before."

"In those days, Gram continued, people couldn't tell the difference between a star and a planet."

"What happened was, three planets, Jupiter, Saturn, and Mercury seemed to come together within the constellation Pisces, or what we call the Fishes. You know some other constellations, like the Big Dipper, The Little Dipper, and you've heard people talk about their Horoscope, or the Zodiac. "Yup," Joe nodded. "You with me, Joe?" asked his Grandmother. Joe nodded his head yes.

Thousands of years ago, many people built towers in their cities so they could get close to the stars. You've heard of the Tower of Babel in Sunday School. Those people gave all the stars names and they felt they all had special meanings, too. One of the planets that seemed to come together within the constellation Fishes, around 6 BC, was Jupiter. It was known as The Star of The Supreme Ruler of The Universe. Saturn, one of the others, was known to those people as The Earthly Representative of The Supreme Ruler. The other was Mercury, known as The Star of Palestine. Pisces was known, among several other things, as the Constellation of The Last Days.

So, the Wise Men gathered from this information, that in the last days, the earthly representative of the supreme ruler of the universe, would be born in Palestine. The religious leaders in Jerusalem told the wise Men that the One they were looking for would be born in Bethlehem, because the prophets had said that's where it would be.

"How do you know all that stuff, Gram, Joe asked her. "I like that kind of stuff, she told him, and I read a lot. For instance, I found an old book that was my grandmothers, that told about finding clay tablets in the ruins of Babylon. They told about everything that was happening in the heavens, and what it all meant to them. They have found at least three clay tablets that record this unusual display in the sky. It's interesting to me to know that at the same time the Wise Men were making records of this on clay tablets, men in Palestine were recording the same things on animal skins.

Some of these records have been found, rolled up and placed in clay jars in caves. They are called.

"It's awfully late, dear," Gram said sleepily, "We need to get to bed, so we can get up for church in the morning." She paused in the middle of the floor, and as an afterthought, said, "I saw a picture of one of the clay tablets I was telling you about, from Babylon, on the internet, not long ago. If we have some time tomorrow, after we get the tree decorated, I'll show it to you."

Gram went over, and gently touched Grampa on his shoulder. "It's bedtime, Carl," she said softly.

"Joe," his grandmother said, "These little baked clay tablets told us everything about the people where the tablets were found." They told us all kinds of things about their neighbors. Most all early civilizations used them. For example the Assyrians had records of somewhere about thirty Jewish kings. One very old empire that went back about six thousand years, and was probably established by a fifth generation grandson of Noah. It was only recently discovered during my lifetime. They had extensive libraries, with dictionary cross referencing four different languages of neighboring civilizations of that time.

This place was named Ebla.

«We know by these cuneiform tablets that the ancient people traded extensively with each other. Pre historic items, for example from Egypt have been found in ruins from pre-ancient Ireland.Trade routes from the Orient carried spices,silk, and tea. Battle shields made from walrus hides, harvested from Greenland, Iceland, and north eastern Canada were preferred by Europeans, because they were light weight, and arrows would not penetrate them. They were traded by Shetlanders made the first seaworthy vessels from whale skeletons.

They would travel to those far off North Sea areas, and stay year ‹round. They would dig holes about the size of our cellars, line them with rocks, turn their boats upside down over them, lash them down, and spend the winters.

Their boats were made of whale skeletons covered with seal skins, and sealed with thick sealer made from walrus fat.

It was interesting to me that the early Shetlanders built tall piles of rocks, and used them as navigational markers.

More interesting to me than the stories on the clay tablets is the fact that these early people were so far advanced in navigation, building, and communication, and not monkeys swinging from the tree tops.

The Babylonian records on their cuneiform tablets were found by an archaeologist telling about King Nebuchadnezzar going insane, and eating grass.

«Not all ancient people wrote on clay tablets» Joe›s grandmother explained. The Egyptians used paper, and their history was mostly painted on the walls of their temples and tombs»

"How did they see in those places to paint so much?" asked Joe.

"Never thought about that Joe", his grandmother said, my guess is they had some kind of reflecting material to reflect sunlight. How long ago was it that you studied about the Egyptians? asked his grandmother. Did the teachers tell you how advanced their engineering was?" Not a lot, " Joe answered, they mentioned that they must have used a lot of slave labor to build the pyramids".

"We haven't been able to figure some of the things they were able to accomplish," she continued. "They built one pyramid, so that one opening from a particular room opens precisely on the North Star!" "Holy cow, exclaimed Joe.

# The Legend Of The Christmas Trees

I haven't thought about all this for years she continued. I need a cup of tea to help me get things straight in my fuzzy mind. Can I fix you a cup of hot chocolate too keep me company doing it? Can I fix you a cup of hot chocolate too keep me company doing it?

What did the three days of darkness mean" Joe asked?" "The Egyptians had several gods in their sun worship", and God showed them Egyptians just who was the mot powerful," she explained.

«I thought it was funny when God sent the frogs, and they hopped into with the Egyptians, and got stuck in the bread dough.»

They must have smelled awful when they all died, Joe added.»

"God didn't fool around with them", said grandmother.

"God showed them," He turned the Nile river red, (blood), He destroyed their crops, killed their livestock, and sent biting insects to torment them.

The Egyptians knew who was doing it too, because they cried out"This is the finger of God!.

«In his book, Harry Rimmer felt sure he had identified the Pharaoh of the Exodus, somewhere between fourteen and fifteen hundred years before Christ, there was a twenty year old son of a Pharaoh buried in the father's tomb Joseph of our Bible was known in Egypt as :The Master Of Hidden Learning", and whenever he went out people were commanded to "Bend The Knee to him

When Moses told the Hebrew people to kill a lamb, sprinkle it›s blood over their door posts, and roast and eat it, it was like killing one of the Egyptian gods.

Joe's grandmother took another sip of tea, and picked up her tea cup.

## The Legend Of The Christmas Trees

We›ve talked about it a little bit this evening,» she said. but they keep finding things that confirm stories in our Bible jut the way it (the Bible) says it did.

One thing very few people really believed was the story of Jonah.

He must have looked like a circus side show freak, after being sloshed around in the belly of a great fish for three days.

For years no one could find the city of Tarshish, so they figured the story wasn't true. However not long ago archaeologist found some beautiful jewelry, in mistakenly made in Tarshish.

There is a picture in an old Book of Knowledge of ruins of a monument in the ruins of Nineveh to Jonah.

In the nineteen eighties, restoration work on the altar that Joshua made on the West Bank of the Jordan river after the Hebrews destroyed Jericho". Joe's grandmother said.

Then Joe cleared his throat, and said: grandmother. Why did God kill all of the people in Jericho, and a lot of the other cities the Hebrews took over. That is hard for me to understand».

"You are right, Joe," grandmother admitted. Many other people have a hard time with it too!".

When you read later on, about the religious stuff that was going on, including child sacrifice, it's easier to understand. I read once that even many animals in that area were infected with horrible diseases. If God had allowed these innocent women and children to live pretty soon the Hebrew people would be doing the same things, and getting many of the same diseases, to.

Records show that later on, the Hebrews were doing some of those things, and God was very displeased.

Joe pondered that for a long time while his grandmother picked up her knitting.

One of the most important finds ever happened in my lifetime since WII" Joe's grandmother told him.

Back in Jesus› lifetime here on earth. There were a number of religions that banded together.

One group of these religious men, called the Essenes spent much of their time copying writings from the profits and ancient historic of Moses and the profits.

When the Roman army was on their way to where the Essenes lived, they sealed the documents they had copied on animal skins, sealed them in clay jars, and hid them in caves near the Dead Sea they have become known as the Dead Sea Scrolls

In thee time since their discovery scholars have translated them. At least parts of every book of our Bible except one, has been found among the scrolls, and to their amazement the writing on these old skins are exactly the same as our Bible today.

As they were going up the stairs to the bedrooms, Joe's grandmother said, "You know Joe, the things you and Grampa told me, that Horace said this morning, about the legend of the Christmas trees, kind of ties in with the star of Bethlehem, doesn't it? Good night, dear."

www.ingramcontent.com/pod-product-compliance
Lightning Source LLC
Chambersburg PA
CBHW030141100526
44592CB00011B/992